MW01143413

The depth of Soul Survivor's experience in youth ministry is finally available for youth groups everywhere! Soul Survivor Encounter utilizes the gospel to energize your students, impassion your leaders and immerse your community in the values of service, relationship, worship, justice and evangelism. Don't miss out on this series of truly fantastic resources!

Josh McDowell
Speaker
Author, *Evidence That Demands a Verdict*

Soul Survivor is undoubtedly in the center of this generation's fresh wind of the Spirit. The message is clear and spiritually motivating. This material is wonderful.

Jim Burns
Founder and President, YouthBuilders

When a devotional starts with quotes from Bono, Avril Lavigne or Mel Gibson, something's up. In the case of Soul Survivor Encounter, that something is starting with youths' real lives, not with a religious subculture. A refreshing mix of classical theology with feet firmly planted in the neighborhood.

Sally Morgenthaler
Speaker
Founder, Sacramentis.com
and Digital Glass Videos

There is no greater challenge facing us today than to engage emerging generations with the truths of the Scriptures, and Soul Survivor Encounter hits the bull's-eye in how to go about doing that.

Dan Kimball
Author, *The Emerging Church: Vintage Christianity for New Generations*
Pastor, Vintage Faith Church
Santa Cruz, California

Soul Survivor is a win-win resource. Youth leaders win with user-friendly resources that bring depth to their ministries. Students win with engaging discussion and reflection tools that help connect the dots between their faith and their life.

Kara Powell
Executive Director, Fuller Seminary Center for Ministry to Youth and Their Families

From the start, Soul Survivor Encounter grabs you and doesn't let go. This new series of materials for students is grounded in the Bible, in touch with the world, full of activities and ideas; a truly interactive thrill for students and their youth leaders!

Darlene Zschech
Worship Leader

Soul Survivor Encounter hits kids where they are on several levels. It is culturally current, interactive, community building and solidly biblical. It brings God's Word right into the teenage world with personal stories, practical application and action steps. It moves from information to transformation and is hip without being flip. With journaling, projects and daily devotions, the Christian life becomes whole, rather than an isolated Sunday experience. Most of all Jesus, the eternal Son of God, is presented as the compelling Lord to be worshiped and a friend to share life with 24/7.

Don Williams, Ph.D.
Speaker
Author, *Twelve Steps with Jesus*

How to Pray for Others

MIKE PILAVACHI
GENERAL EDITOR

Gospel Light

Gospel Light is a Christian publisher
dedicated to serving the local church. We believe
God's vision for Gospel Light is to provide church
leaders with biblical, user-friendly materials that
will help them evangelize, disciple and minister
to children, youth and families.

It is our prayer that this Gospel Light resource
will help you discover biblical truth for your
own life and help you minister to youth.
May God richly bless you.

*For a free catalog of resources from Gospel Light,
please contact your Christian supplier or contact us at*
1-800-4-GOSPEL *or* www.gospellight.com.

PUBLISHING STAFF
William T. Greig, Chairman
Dr. Elmer L. Towns, Senior Consulting Publisher
Natalie Clark, Product Line Manager
Pam Weston, Managing Editor
Alex Field, Associate Editor
Jessie Minassian, Editorial Assistant
Bayard Taylor, M.Div., Senior Editor,
Biblical and Theological Issues
Mike Pilavachi, General Editor
**Aaron Adams, Gareth Dickinson, Ali MacInnes, Lis
Biddulph, Tim Hughes** and **Pete Hughes,** Contributors
Samantha Hsu, Art Director
Zelle Olson, Designer

ISBN 0-8307-3527-5
© 2004 Gospel Light
All rights reserved.
Printed in the U.S.A.

Scripture quotations are taken from the *Holy Bible, New International
Version*®. Copyright © 1973, 1978, 1984 by International Bible Society.
Used by permission of Zondervan Publishing House. All rights reserved.

contents

introduction

Soul Survivor is committed to equipping young people to make a difference in the world for the kingdom of God. We believe that God is bringing up a new generation of young leaders who want to impact their homes, schools, work and community for Him. Over the past 10 years, we've watched individuals from around the world express their passion and devotion for God in so many different ways. Whether it's through worship, the arts, evangelism, social justice or another avenue entirely, we realize how powerfully God is working in this generation of believers.

One of the incredible ways we've seen young people make a difference for God in the lives of others has been through prayer ministry. The purpose of this booklet is to provide youth leaders with a guide for conducting prayer ministry in their own group. These guidelines are based on biblical principles and the ministry experience gained at Soul Survivor meetings and events. Our goal is not only to encourage leaders to pray for their students but also to encourage students to pray for each other and move forward into leadership roles.

The model of prayer ministry outlined in these pages is not the only model being used by God today. That said, however, this model has worked fantastically for Soul Survivor and we are excited to share it with you. No matter your specific area of ministry or your reason for purchasing this book, our hope is that its content will challenge, inspire and equip you to serve God and those around you through the ministry of prayer.

CHAPTER ONE

BIBLICAL BASIS

If you cracked open your Bible and read a bit through the Gospels, there's a pretty good chance that you'd run into something about Jesus and what He called the "kingdom of God" (Luke 9:2). The kingdom was a big deal to Jesus. Wherever He went, He brought with Him a new way of living life, of relating to God and of connecting with others. He brought with Him "the kingdom of heaven" (Matthew 3:2).

So what do we see as a result of Jesus' having opened the door to this new way of life? We see that He loved the unloved. We see His passion for those who were far from His Father. We see that He was dedicated to living a holy life. And if we read even a tiny bit of the Gospels, we see that He performed miracles and healings. If

Jesus brought with Him the kingdom of God, then these amazing moments are part of living in that kingdom.

Matthew, Mark, Luke and John recorded what happened during Jesus' life and ministry here on Earth. It's pretty obvious that to these men Jesus' miracles and healings were an important part of who He was and what He did. Sometimes when we read about Jesus' miracles we come away amazed. But simple amazement wasn't the purpose behind the miracles and healings of Jesus. His goal wasn't just to shock people.

Have you ever wondered why Jesus got so frustrated with the people He met who asked Him to perform a miracle (see Mark 8:11-12)? He was frustrated because the miracle wasn't the point! The miracles of Jesus are all signs that point to an all-powerful God who is passionately in love with humanity. Like the love He showed, the words He preached, the life He lived and the way He served, His miracles are signs of the arrival of the kingdom of God—a place where the broken are mended and the suffering are freed for the sake of love.

The following chart is a list of Scripture passages that tell the story of many of Jesus' miracles:

	Matthew	Mark	Luke	John
Jesus feeds 5,000 people	14:15-21	6:35-44	9:12-17	6:5-13
Jesus calms the storm	8:23-27	4:35-41	8:22-25	
Demons are sent into pigs	8:28-34	5:1-20	8:26-39	
Jairus's daughter is raised	9:18-19, 23-26	5:22-24,35-43	8:41-42;49-56	
A sick woman is healed	9:20-22	5:25-34	8:43-48	
Jesus heals a paralytic	9:1-8	2:1-12	5:17-26	
A leper is healed	8:1-4	1:40-45	5:12-14	
Peter's mother-in-law is healed	8:14-17	1:29-31	4:38-39	
A shriveled hand is restored	12:9-14	3:1-6	6:6-10	
A boy with an evil spirit is healed	17:14-18	9:14-27	9:38-42	
Jesus walks on the water	14:22-33	6:45-52		6:16-21
Blind Bartimaeus receives sight	20:29-34	10:46-52	18:35-43	
A girl is freed from demon possession	15:21-28	7:24-30		
Jesus feeds 4,000 people	15:32-38	8:1-9		
A centurion's servant is healed	8:5-13		7:1-9	
An evil spirit is sent out of a man		1:23-27	4:33-36	
A mute healed and freed of a demon	12:22	11:14-15		

	Matthew	Mark	Luke	John
Two blind men find sight	9:27-31			
Jesus heals the mute man	9:32-34			
A coin in a fish's mouth	17:24-27			
A deaf and mute man is healed		7:32-35		
A blind man sees at Bethsaida		8:22-26		
Jesus performs miraculous catch of fish			5:1-11	
A widow's son is raised			7:11-15	
A crippled woman is healed			13:10-13	
Jesus heals a sick man			14:1-4	
Ten lepers are healed			17:11-19	
Jesus restores a man's ear			22:49-51	18:10-11
Jesus turns water into wine				2:1-10
An official's son is healed at Cana				4:46-53
A lame man is healed				5:1-15
Jesus heals a man born blind				9:1-38
Lazarus is raised from the dead				11:1-44
Jesus performs a second miraculous catch of fish				21:1-13

Jesus brought with Him a new kingdom that was different from anything that had come before. His miracles ushered in that kingdom and made it clear to those who recognized it that God was doing a new thing. But while Jesus came to show His Father's love through these signs and wonders, He was also demonstrating the power the kingdom of God had over illness, nature and Satan himself. The kingdom Jesus brought was the perfect balance of absolute love and absolute power.

> When Jesus had called the Twelve together, he gave them power and authority to drive out all demons and to cure diseases, and he sent them out to preach the kingdom of God and to heal the sick (Luke 9:1-2).

In Matthew 28:18-20 and Luke 10:1-24, Jesus called together His followers and commissioned them to continue the work of God's kingdom. This meant that they were to share the truth of Jesus with others as they followed His model of living.

It's also very clear from these verses that they were to follow in His work of teaching, baptizing, healing and performing miracles. And remember: The call Jesus gave to His disciples over 2,000 years ago still speaks to us today. As His modern-day followers, we can take part in all God's kingdom has to offer—acts of love, words of truth, passion for service, the life of holiness and a ministry of power.

CHAPTER TWO

VALUES AND BELIEFS

In the same way that a coach's philosophy drives his team's performance, a ministry's values and beliefs drive its strategy for outreach. For example, if a football or basketball coach values offense, he will focus his team on the task of scoring. If the coach values defense, his team will be fired up to keep their opponents from scoring.

Values and beliefs shape the way a person acts. If someone values time with his or her friends, there's a good chance that person won't turn down offers to go to the movies with them. If a family believes in the importance of education, the parents will make sure their children keep up with their studies.

Before moving into a discussion about how to do prayer ministry, we need to know the kinds of things that are important to us as Christians—we need to know our beliefs. If we don't know our beliefs or values, we'll go through life like ships drifting aimlessly on the ocean. In other words, values give us direction.

The Cross of Christ

For the message of the cross is foolishness to those who are perishing, but to us who are being saved it is the power of God.
1 Corinthians 1:18

It's no mistake that the Cross is the most visible symbol of Christianity in the world today. It's at the center of what we believe as Christians. When we say, "We are Christians," we're saying that we believe the Cross was more than just the method of execution of some radical preacher 2,000 years ago. We're saying that on that day the world and everything in it was changed forever. To those who believe in Jesus, the Cross represents forgiveness of sins and the opportunity to live a new kind of life with God. The Cross brought us *freedom*.

Freedom from Lies

As we read the Bible, it becomes clear right away that Satan is out to lie to humanity—to destroy us by hiding the truth (see John 8:44). But what's his plan? He'll make us believe that we can find all the answers in things like money, fame, power and self-satisfaction. The Cross has torn all that away and pointed us to the fact that the ultimate truth is found in the ultimate sacrifice—the sacrifice of God's own Son.

Freedom from Fear

Paul put it best in Romans 8:15 when he wrote, "For you did not receive a spirit that makes you a slave again to fear, but you received the Spirit of sonship. And by him we cry, 'Abba, Father.'" Paul is saying that through Jesus' sacrifice we have been brought into the family of God. We are no longer alone and we aren't responsible for fighting our own battles. We have nothing to fear. We only need to cry out for our Father. A good father—and we have the best in God—is there to love, protect and guide his children.

Freedom from Sin

Have you ever popped in your favorite CD, sung along with the first few lines and stopped in horror when the music skipped, replaying the same clip of music over and over again? It's not long before you have to make the choice between stopping the CD or going absolutely crazy. That's kind of how life is in relationship to sin as we make the same mistakes again and again. We go down the wrong path time after time, and it can drive us mad! At the Cross we find that we are no longer slaves to sin. We are forgiven our past and given a new hope for our future. Paul put it this way: "For we know that our old self was crucified with him so that the body of sin might be done away with, that we should no longer be slaves to sin" (Romans 6:6).

It must have been horrible for those who loved Jesus to see Him hanging up on the cross that day. Despite the ugliness of that day, something truly wonderful was being born. Jesus' sacrifice on the cross allows us to have confidence and security as we come to God for ourselves and for those we care about. Through His pain and sacrifice we have been made whole. We have been made His sons and daughters. We have been given power and been set free.

THE WORD OF GOD

All Scripture is God-breathed and is useful for teaching, rebuking, correcting and training in righteousness, so that the man of God may be thoroughly equipped for every good work.
2 Timothy 3:16-17

Have you ever been in a car with someone who is completely lost but who refuses to pull over and ask for directions? You offer to get out the map, but he or she refuses, saying "No. No. No. I know where I'm going. I think it's just a bit further up this road." You sigh and lean back in your seat, knowing it will be a while before you get anywhere.

Similarly, we can spend a long time wandering around in our Christian life if we don't get direction from the Bible. Any person or ministry that doesn't ground itself in what the Word of God has to say is going to end up traveling down the wrong road. Everything we do and everything we believe comes out of the truth in Scripture.

It's like putting together a puzzle with young children. They get a few pieces in the right place but get carried away and try to make a piece fit where it doesn't belong. They bang the piece with their fists. They flip it around. They scrunch up their faces in frustration but the piece just doesn't fit. Similarly, we can try to make our ministries work. We can try to make our relationships work. We can try to make our lives work. But everything will be out of place if what we're doing doesn't agree with what the Bible says. In prayer ministry it's the Bible that reminds us of our authority for healing, shows us how to do things, helps us to avoid hype and warns us against wrong motives. Just like the children and the puzzle, we can't make up our own rules about how things should work. God has set the standard and He's recorded it in the pages of the Bible. The standard doesn't change to fit us; instead, we must change to fit the standard.

THE HOLY SPIRIT

The Spirit helps us in our weakness. We do not know what we ought to pray for, but the Spirit himself intercedes for us with groans that words cannot express.

Romans 8:26

Have you ever started making your favorite meal or dessert and somewhere in the process realized that you didn't have all the necessary ingredients? Depending on how far along you are, you may try to use some kind of substitute, hoping the dish will pass as edible, but most of the time you can tell that something's missing. The flavor just isn't there. It's too sweet or its texture feels wrong.

In the busyness of our lives, sometimes we leave out the Person and work of the Holy Spirit. We may be able to get along for a while and our ministries may even see results. But without the Holy Spirit, our work can't ever be complete. God doesn't intend for ministry to be this way.

For many, the Holy Spirit's role in our lives is mysterious. However, the Bible makes it clear that He is real and His work is essential to living the lives God has called us to live. The following descriptions are just a few of the characteristics of the Holy Spirit as found in Scripture:

- The Holy Spirit is God's agent for bringing new life. "The Spirit gives life; the flesh counts for nothing" (John 6:63).

- The Holy Spirit directs the Church. "While they were worshiping the Lord and fasting, the

Holy Spirit said, 'Set apart for me Barnabas and Saul for the work to which I have called them'" (Acts 13:2). "He who has an ear, let him hear what the Spirit says to the churches" (Revelation 2:7).

- The Holy Spirit teaches us the things of God the Father. "But when he, the Spirit of truth, comes, he will guide you into all truth. He will not speak on his own; he will speak only what he hears, and he will tell you what is yet to come" (John 16:13).

- The Holy Spirit will always give the glory to Jesus. "[The Holy Spirit] will bring glory to [Jesus] by taking from what is [His] and making it known to you" (John 16:14).

- The Holy Spirit administers spiritual gifts. "All these are the work of one and the same Spirit, and he gives them to each one, just as he determines" (1 Corinthians 12:11).

- The Holy Spirit brings about healing in the name of Jesus. "I will not venture to speak of anything except what Christ has accomplished through me in leading the Gentiles to obey God by what I have said and done—by the power of signs and miracles, through the power of the Spirit" (Romans 15:18-19).

THE VALUE OF THE INDIVIDUAL

A pastor once told the true story of a construction worker who fell from a ladder to the ground below. A bar of steel sticking up from the ground pierced his body as he fell. Amazingly, the man survived the ordeal and remained awake and aware the whole time.

A crowd quickly gathered around the terrible sight, and emergency professionals were called to the scene. Rescue workers freed the man and rushed him to the hospital. As unbelievable as it may be, the man survived the awful accident. He was interviewed later and asked what he was thinking and feeling while he waited to be rescued.

He responded by saying that he had never felt so alone in his life.

It's hard to believe, isn't it? On the scene, emergency workers were tending to his needs, a crowd of people had gathered around him, and news reporters stood nearby taking notes. In the midst of all this, he felt alone?

In another way, it makes complete sense. We've all been in a crowd of people and felt alone. We've all been surrounded by others and had the nagging feeling that we didn't matter. It's important for us at Soul Survivor that in prayer ministry, each individual who comes for prayer leaves knowing he or she is loved, assured that he or she is not alone.

We believe that God lovingly created every person; therefore, we must treat each person with dignity and respect. When we come in contact with others, we must see God in them and treat them accordingly.

In times of prayer ministry, it's important to realize that the person for whom we're praying is special. Each person has a unique story, has unique needs and deserves our full attention. It is important that, as we minister to each person, he or she doesn't feel alone or embarrassed. We must do everything we can to protect the dignity of every person with whom we pray. The following guidelines will help you do just that:

- We do not say that prayer or prayer ministry isn't working for the person with whom we're praying.

- We do not say that someone is sinful, possessed by a demon or lacking in faith.

- When someone confesses sin, we do not react with shock or disgust.

- When someone confesses sin, we never share that confession with others.

- After praying with someone, it's important that that person knows that he or she is loved even if he or she leaves with nothing else!

THE BODY OF CHRIST

Humans have always been interested in the stars. Over time, scientists and astronomers have helped us understand more and more the reality of what's going on out there. Today, people with enough money have even been able to buy their own ticket to fly into outer space. The worlds of science fiction books and movies are finally coming to life!

It's amazing to think that many years ago almost everyone believed that the sun, moon and planets all rotated around planet Earth. Foolish though it seems now, the men and women of that time firmly believed that Earth was the center of the universe.

It's a sad fact, but each of us is capable of making the same mistake. It's too easy to think that others in our universe—our friends, family and coworkers—all revolve around us. We may fall into a trap by thinking, *I don't need everyone else. Everyone else needs me* or *If it's going to get done, it needs to get done my way.*

Paul provided us with the best illustration of our dependence on one another when he described us as different parts of the Body, working together as God called us.

> Now the body is not made up of one part but of many. If the foot should say, "Because I am not a hand, I do not belong to the body," it would not for that reason cease to be part of the body. And if the ear should say, "Because I am not an eye, I do not belong to the body," it would not for that reason cease to be part of the body. If the whole body were an eye, where would the sense of hearing be? If the whole body were an ear, where would the sense of smell be? But in fact God has arranged the parts in the body, every one of them, just as he wanted them to be. If they were all one

part, where would the body be? As it is, there are many parts, but one body (1 Corinthians 12:14-20).

That says it all. We need each other. God commands that we live together in love and peace with one another (see John 13:35; Ephesians 4:3). The Body of Christ influences our prayer ministry in the following ways:

- We practice forgiveness, peace and love for the Body of Christ in our lives so that we can minister from a place of integrity and wholeness.

- When it is appropriate, we encourage those who have been hurt and wronged to forgive as Christ has forgiven us.

- We never insist that one particular way of doing prayer ministry is the only way God works.

- We remember that prayer ministry is part of our service to God and to others; it is not a one-person show.

CHAPTER THREE

GUIDELINES

CORPORATE MINISTRY

Maybe you've been to an event or a meeting at which the speaker makes a general call for people to come forward for prayer. In these times people may be encouraged to be open to the work of the Holy Spirit. Those who come forward may not be responding to a specific issue but may be coming forward to receive something from the Lord.

As you minister to those who come forward, one of the most important things to remember is that this is a time to let God do His own thing. Try not to get in the way of what He has already begun. Instead, try to help people focus on the Lord and encourage them to take in what He is doing at that moment.

It's important to be patient and to avoid being too enthusiastic. Remember that it's not about you. You're there to partner with someone as he or she comes before God to receive. You're there to hear what the Father is saying. You're there to try to understand what part He wants you to play as He works in the person's life. Some of the following comments may help you encourage people in this process:

- "I bless what God is doing."

- "Focus on the Lord."

- "Go on receiving."

- "The Holy Spirit is on you."

As you pay attention to God and to the individual with whom you're praying, also pay attention to what is being said by the leaders in front. As they listen to God, it's important that you hear what God is saying to them and see how it may apply to what God is doing in the life of the person with whom you're praying.

Remember that you are there to help, support and encourage the person as he or she meets with God. There's no need to rush what is happening, because you're

not making it happen. Simply bless someone and move on. It's important to listen.
Listen to the person with whom you're
praying as well as to the leaders God has
given you. Above all else, listen to God,
and be sensitive to how He may want to
use you.

INDIVIDUAL MINISTRY

There are times when it's necessary to
spend a longer period of time ministering
to an individual. Perhaps there has been a
specific call from a speaker or leader.
Maybe the person for whom you're praying begins to show more powerful outward expressions of God's working. In
these kinds of situations, remain aware of
what is happening and listen intently for
what God may be saying.

In individual ministry, as with corporate ministry, it's very important to
remember that the work going on in someone's life is the result of God's work and
not your own. Your job is to be with the
person as he or she connects with God.
Allow God to work through you in any way
He desires. Always point your journey
toward Christ, and allow yourself to be led
by the Holy Spirit in the process.

While there are some similarities between corporate and individual ministry, there are also some important differences to think about. As you spend more time with the person, dive a bit deeper. Discover more about what the person is looking for from the Lord. Think about conducting prayer ministry as though you were a waiter or waitress. Like a waiter or waitress, you take the order and deliver it to the chef. You don't mix the ingredients. You don't cook it just the right way. You don't take it from the oven or arrange the dish so that it's aesthetically pleasing. Just as you would take the order and deliver it to the chef, in individual prayer ministry, you listen to the needs of the person to whom you're ministering and simply help deliver those needs to God. He fills the order. As a matter of fact, He already has the oven heated and the ingredients mixed. The following guidelines are insights and steps for individual prayer ministry:

- Keep in mind that at least one person ministering must be of the same sex as the individual being prayed for.

- Ask each person what he or she would like prayer for.

- Remember the importance of treating each person with love and dignity; truly listen to the person with whom you're praying.

- Listen to what the Lord is saying as you minister to the individual.

- Invite the Holy Spirit to come as you pray together.

- Remember to guide and encourage each person as he or she presses on to what God has for him or her.

- Remember to practice patience. It's God's work and not yours.

- When it's appropriate, ask the person about what God may be doing at that time.

- Never act shocked, disappointed or upset by what anyone else may share with you.

- Keep confidential the things that are shared with you in ministry time.

- Remember the priority of forgiveness; recognize the need for others to forgive and to be forgiven.

- Realize that it's okay to express emotion when God works in your life.

- If God gives you a word of knowledge, prophecy, revelation or a picture to speak, you may begin by praying along those lines. When you do offer what you believe God has given, do so in a way that allows the person the freedom to either accept or reject it. Never insist that the word is from God. Have the humility to realize that you could be wrong.

- Laying hands on another person is a biblical step for blessing and healing. Before you lay your hands on someone, ask permission and be sensitive as to where you place your hands.

- If someone begins to show outward signs of God's work through physical response or the gift of tongues, help calm any fears or embarrassment he or she may be feeling. Offer encouragement by saying something along the lines of "Don't be afraid," "It's okay to receive," "You can stop any time but try to go with it" or "The Lord is at work—He loves you."

- Remember that you are part of the Body of Christ and under the authority of the pastor, team leader or speaker at a service or meeting.

- Never set up a time to meet with a person outside of the ministry time. We don't want to build a dependent relationship or open the door to any difficult situations. Always remember that prayer ministry is not counseling; and if someone needs those services, help him or her find a counselor.

- Never tell a person that he or she has a demon or evil spirit. You could be wrong and it may unnecessarily scare the individual. The focus for prayer is always Jesus, not the demonic. However, do recognize the very real existence of demons and evil spirits. Though it is not common, if you sense a demon may be present or manifesting, ask an experienced member of the ministry team to join you. As in all cases, remember that the dignity of the individual is paramount.

HEALING PRAYER

Often, individual prayer ministry will happen in response to a spiritual or emotional need. But there are times when ministry is a response to a need for physical healing. In these situations we suggest the following:

- Ask, "Where does it hurt?" Specific information may be too personal to share and that is okay, so don't push the question.

- Invite the Holy Spirit to come in the name of Jesus.

- Ask God to bring healing in the name of Jesus.

- If it is appropriate and after asking permission, lay hands on the part of the body where it hurts.

- As you pray, it's important to remember the authority God has given you to pray for healing in the name of Jesus and through the power of the Holy Spirit. Simply pray that God would heal the body. Some prayer leaders may want to speak directly to the condition.

- Pray for wisdom and discernment from God. In some cases, emotional hurt or sin could be the root of the physical problems.

- Bless what God is doing and ask Him to increase His healing power.

- When the time is right, you might ask the person if he or she feels anything different.

- Continue to pray for healing if the person has not felt any release.

- Do not suggest to anyone that he or she stop taking any medical treatment. That is the place of those in the medical profession whom God also uses to bring healing.

Prayer for healing may have the following outcomes:

- Immediate healing—Be thankful, praise God and give Him the glory.

- Delayed healing—Read the story of the 10 lepers in Luke 17:11-17.

- Partial healing—Read the story of the blind man in Mark 8:22-25. In this case you might want to continue to pray for complete healing.

- No apparent healing—Don't say someone is healed if he or she is not. Sometimes that's just the way God works. Trust Him, for He is faithful.

TEAM SUPPORT

Finally, it is important to realize when you need support. Prayer ministry is never a one-person show, and there are times when you'll need to seek out the guidance and wisdom of others. If you begin to feel uncomfortable, ask another team member to join you and help.

You need to contact a leader if there is a reported instance of physical or sexual abuse. Anyone who shares this kind of information should be treated with sensitive support, and it is best if more than one person joins in this kind of ministry.

If the abuse is from the past, address it as a deep wound and allow this person a safe place for expressing that pain. It is important to help this individual recognize that the responsibility lies not with him or her but with the abuser. At that point the person can begin the healing process through forgiveness, eventually finding release from the burden of guilt and shame. Always remember that this kind of healing is a process that takes time. Try not to force the issue ahead of what God is doing.

If the abuse is current, immediately contact a leader for prayer ministry. Local laws may require than an instance of current abuse be reported to the proper law-enforcement authorities. Healing from physical or emotional abuse may also require ongoing Christian counseling.

CHAPTER FOUR

PRAYER MINISTRY ISSUES

FORGIVING THE PAST

Jesus once told a great story about a man who owed his boss a huge amount of money (see Matthew 18:21-35). The employer brought the man before him and demanded payment. Leaving all his dignity at the door, the man threw himself on the ground and begged for mercy and more time to get the money together. The boss was moved by the man's passion and not only agreed to let him off the hook but also canceled the entire debt.

As the man left, most likely thanking heaven for his good fortune, he ran into a fellow employee who owed him a small amount of money. He seized his coworker by the throat and began to choke him, demanding his money back. When he realized that the fellow worker couldn't pay him back, the man had his coworker thrown in jail.

His fellow employees had witnessed the whole thing and were so upset by the situation that they scheduled an appointment with their boss to let him know the disturbing details. It wasn't long before the man once again found himself in his boss's office. The employer angrily expressed his disbelief that a man who had just been freed from the weight of a huge debt would walk out the door and that very same day throw another person in jail over a small amount of money.

His employer was through with him. He turned the man over to the prison jailers, making sure they knew to hold him until he had paid his debt in full. In this story, Jesus' message of forgiveness is very clear. But His point is both an invitation and a challenge.

We see the heart of a God who loves us so much that He is willing to forgive even the largest of debts. The story shows us that no matter what we've done, God has a heart of compassion, forgiving those who go to Him with an honest spirit of sorrow and repentance. We need only receive this amazing gift through prayer. Many people find it helpful to pray with someone else when going before God and asking forgiveness.

In the story, we also see a God who asks that we forgive others as we have been forgiven. To God, no debt on Earth can compare to the one His Son paid when He died on the cross. The boss's angry response is God's challenge to each of us to live by the same standard of compassion and forgiveness that He has shown. However, it's more than just a challenge—God commands us to forgive one another in the same way that He forgives us when we go to Him in repentance (see Mark 11:25). He knows that when we forgive others, we become more like Him. He knows that when we forgive, we release our own burdens from the past and make a first step toward restoring broken relationships. As we work toward forgiveness, it is important to remember that it's a process that often takes time and effort to complete.

Sometimes we may be unsure of the source of our anger or hurt. Pain or anger may have been covered up by years of denial or bitterness. Here we need to ask for God's help to reveal the source of the pain being experienced. We should feel free to express those feelings to God—He is always willing to hear honest words coming from broken hearts. We then want to move toward forgiving the person who caused us pain, asking God to forgive him or her too. If the Lord convicts us of harboring unnecessary anger, bitterness or resentment, we might also ask the Lord's forgiveness for these attitudes. Finally, we need to ask the Holy Spirit to come and seal the process by healing the hurt that may remain.

Wounds don't heal overnight, but thankfully God's grace is truly amazing. It is a free gift given from our Father's heart. We're forgiven not because we deserve it but because we are the children of God. However, to truly receive grace the way God intends it, we must also forgive those who have hurt us. By doing that, we're acting in obedience to God while also living life free from the bonds of our past.

GIVING A PRAYER OF INVITATION

It's happened to everyone. You're hanging out with friends, and you all decide to go out to grab a bite to eat. After about five minutes, it becomes painfully clear that no one in the group is willing to make a decision on where to go. Chinese? Curry? Pizza? Mexican? After an awkward silence, several near fistfights and a few angry words, someone will suggest a restaurant that's on nobody's list of favorites. At this point you're all too tired to care anymore, so everyone goes along.

It can be annoying when too many heads collide when making insignificant decisions such as where to eat dinner or what movie to see. On the other hand, most of us would agree that when it comes to making big decisions we listen to what our friends have to say. There aren't many people who would choose between two incredible jobs without calling their best mate to ask what he or she thinks. Usually when choosing what university to attend, students will talk about it with trusted friends and family before making a decision. When making big choices, we want others to support us and to help make sense of it all.

There's no bigger decision in life than the decision to follow Christ. It's the choice between life and death, between hope and hopelessness. In prayer ministry, there will be times when an individual responds to a call to make Christ the center of his or her life. Like with other ministry situations discussed in this book, you don't want to rush to the end or get too anxious to get to the good stuff.

It's helpful to go over the details of what it means to be a Christian and try to determine what motivated the individual to make this decision at this time. Some might have followed their friends or were moved emotionally, and they may not have a firm grasp on the decision. While they may not be in the best place to take that next step, it's important to give them an opportunity to make a commitment to Jesus. Whatever the motivation, it's always a good idea to go over the key points of the Christian message. There isn't just *one way* to describe the story of salvation. But the best way to describe a life of following Jesus is simply by being you. You don't need to give a university lecture on theological doctrines; instead, you can take this opportunity to express what Christ means to you. Just look at the variety of methods God used to bring people to Him in the Bible. The following ideas are some of the keys to explaining the Christian faith:

- If we are left to live life alone, we'll be stuck in a pattern of sin that we can never get out of (see Romans 3:23).

- In spite of everything, God has an amazing and passionate love for us (see John 3:16).

- To express His love, Jesus became one of us, lived a perfect life as an example and died on the cross to free us from our sin and provide us with the opportunity for an amazing relationship with God (see 1 Peter 3:18).

- We have the opportunity to respond to God's love for us by making an important decision to follow Him.

Just as there isn't *one way* to explain our faith, there isn't *one prayer* to become a Christian. However, most would agree that the Bible outlines some important steps we need to take to move forward into a new life with Him.

- First, we confess our sin to Him, trusting that He will forgive us without question because of what Jesus did on the cross.

- Next, we express our belief in what Jesus did through His death and resurrection.

- Finally, we invite God to take charge of our lives, committing ourselves to living life the way He intends.

Sometimes a speaker or leader will lead in this kind of prayer. Other times, after explaining the decision, you may want to have the person repeat the prayer after you. There are times when the person may pray out loud and times when the person may pray in silence. Whatever the case, remember that this is an incredibly sacred and personal moment between that person and God. You are there to act as God's assistant, doing only what He asks. You are there to support, encourage and guide the person through the process.

As you finish your time with the individual, pray for the person and ask God to fill him or her with the Holy Spirit, sealing what He has done. Remember that this is a time to rejoice with and encourage the individual in his or her newfound faith. Make sure there is a local church that the person can attend on a regular basis to help build a growing relationship with God.

INVITING THE HOLY SPIRIT

Most children and even some adults can't handle the idea of an unopened present. Some parents consider hiring full-time security to make sure they don't arrive home from work one day to find that the floor beneath the Christmas tree has been looted. Children often beg and plead with

their parents to allow them to open their gifts early. They insist that making them wait is cruel and unusual punishment and a violation of the law.

There are times when a parent will give in and let the child open his or her presents before a birthday or Christmas has arrived. It's fun for the moment; after all, who doesn't like to receive gifts? Still, it's pretty hard to wake up on your birthday or on Christmas Day knowing that you have no presents to open. Lying there in bed, the child promises not to open any presents early again—at least not until next year.

Patience is a difficult thing for young and old. Today, we're surrounded by fast food, high-speed Internet access and delivery services that bring groceries to our front door. In ministry time, however, we put a strong emphasis on waiting and working through the power of the Holy Spirit. While most of us like the part about working in the power of the Holy Spirit, the waiting for Him to work can sometimes be another matter.

When you invite the Holy Spirit to come as you minister to someone, it's important to communicate both inwardly and outwardly that you are ready to wait for Him to arrive in His own way. You don't need to fill the silence with words. There's nothing worse than watching a beautiful sunset or sitting on top of a rolling green hillside with a person who's talking nonstop. These are times to honor God in silence.

Often, waiting for the Holy Spirit can be one of those times. You may want to say a few words or nothing at all. You need to

simply wait, listen and watch for the Spirit to do what He wants. As you wait, it's important to remember that the Holy Spirit works in many ways. He may work in one way at a large conference but then do something entirely different at a local church meeting or home Bible study.

Remember to trust the Spirit more than you trust yourself. First off, do you trust that if you ask Him, the Holy Spirit will come? In Luke 11:13, Jesus made it clear that God will send the Holy Spirit to those who ask. You don't need to warm Him up to come to you. The moment you ask, He's on His way. Second, do you trust that the Holy Spirit knows how to work in the life of the person with whom you're praying? It can be encouraging to see outward signs of the Holy Spirit's work in someone's life, but it's important that you are just as confident that the Holy Spirit has worked when there is no outward display at all.

It's clear that the Holy Spirit is God's agent of power and change. We must call on Him as we minister to others. As we do so, we must be confident that our Father has indeed heard our request and that the Holy Spirit is already at work in the best way possible.

CHAPTER FIVE

THE SPIRITUAL GIFTS

Followers of Christ hailing from different backgrounds approach the subject of spiritual gifts in various ways. In this chapter we will discuss how we have seen the Holy Spirit work at Soul Survivor. Obviously, it's important for you to take these ideas and principles and apply them how you see fit.

THE GIFT OF PROPHECY

"Guaranteed Weight-Loss Program!"

"Buy Your Favorite Music
for the Lowest Price Ever!"

"Win a New Car Today!"

"Collectible Gold-Plated
Kitty-Kat Spoons—Click Here!"

It's awful to have to clean out a fresh load of junk mail from your e-mail account. But sometimes in the middle of all the mess, you'll see an e-mail address you recognize. One click and you can catch up with a friend you saw last night or even last year. And minutes later, you can send an e-mail to your friend whether your friend lives around the corner or all the way around the world.

Only a few years ago you had to have a pen, paper and envelope to connect with someone who lived any distance away. Today, there are more ways to communicate with people than ever before: mail, phone, e-mail, text messages and instant messages. Fifteen years from now that list will probably double in size.

It's always been that way with God. For thousands of years He's connected with

humanity in many ways. We hear the words of God through Bible study, prayer, sermons, teachings and through the beauty and wonder of creation around us. There are also times when we hear the words of God through the mouths of other people. This is called prophecy. To put it very simply, prophecy is another way God has chosen to talk to His people.

We want to make it very clear, however, that God has also spoken to this world through His Word, the Bible. The Bible is the definitive authority of God on Earth by which all other forms of revelation or prophecy must be measured. The primary difference between the Bible and the gift of prophecy is simple: The Bible is the universal and authoritative Word of God for all of humanity, while prophecy, as referred to in the New Testament, is more specific to time and place in its application. And no prophecy should be spoken if it contradicts the Bible.

God can choose any means He desires in order to speak to us. It is truly amazing that He allows us to be used through the gift of prophecy. Paul tells us in 1 Corinthians 14:1 that we should seek after all spiritual gifts but we should especially seek the gift of prophecy. To speak a message from God—there is hardly a greater honor or greater responsibility.

It's important that we know the purpose behind prophecy. What does the Bible have to say about prophecy in action? We should keep the following points in mind as we discuss this gift:

- God gave the gift of prophecy to Daniel in the Old Testament and He can do the same thing today (see Daniel 1:17).

- Prophecy reveals God's intentions and plans to His people (see Amos 3:7).

- The purpose of prophecy is to build, encourage and strengthen the Church (see 1 Corinthians 14:3-5).

- Prophecy can draw an unbeliever to God (see 1 Corinthians 14:24-25).

- God promised that the gift of prophecy would be widely experienced by the Church (see Joel 2:28; Acts 2:17-21).

- Prophecy points to Jesus (see Revelation 19:10).

As we said earlier, we should desire the gift of prophecy and learn to exercise it when given the opportunity. However, we must always be guided by the principles of godly love and humility. Love ensures that our motives are always for the good of others. We aren't out to make a name for ourselves. We're not out to say something that builds us up while tearing someone else down. Humility helps us keep perspective as we exercise this gift. If we are humble, then we know that we're simply honored messengers of the King. If we are humble, we'll allow others to weigh the words we feel God has given to us without taking offense (see 1 Corinthians 14:29). As we begin to ask God for this amazing gift, we would also do well to ask that He anchor it with love and humility.

A prophetic word can be given to us in a variety of ways. In the Bible, men and women receive prophetic messages from God through visions, nature, dreams, worship and impressions. God may ask us to speak on His behalf during a worship service. We may receive a word, picture or impression during a time of prayer or Scripture reading. God may even surprise us and give us a message when we least expect it.

For some of us, when someone mentions the word "prophet," our mind automatically jumps to a picture of an old man with a beard down to his ankles, yelling about something or other. Granted, there have been some like that, but we need to realize that prophecy can also be a very regular kind of occurrence. After all, it's based on the idea that we're hearing from God and doing His will, both of which should be very basic parts of the Christian life.

When giving a prophetic word to an individual, there's no need to try out your special *God voice* on the person for whom you're praying. Listen for God's voice, because you never want to rush into giving a prophetic message. Try to speak as you always do, as if passing along a phone message for your brother or sister. The message may be long, it may be short, it may be complete, or it may be partial. There are even times when a word may have no specific meaning when it is given but will become relevant in the future. Whatever does happen, remember that you should remain positive. The word should always steer toward the loving-kindness of God. Offer it humbly—knowing the person needs to weigh whether it is from the Lord.

If you give a prophetic message to someone, it's helpful if you can help him or her to receive, weigh or respond to the word. Encourage the person with whom you're praying to follow some of these steps during and after the ministry time.

- Be comfortable with the idea that you can actually expect to receive and pass on messages from God.

Also, know that men and women can make mistakes in speaking these words.

- Ask God for direction and help: "God, what are you saying to me here?"

- Make sure the word doesn't contradict Scripture.

- Ask yourself if there might be other motives or emotions, such as anger, pride or frustration, in the message you received.

- Ask yourself if the prophecy glorifies Jesus or brings us closer to God.

- Prophecy should always strengthen, encourage and comfort.

In the end, the real focus of all of God's messages to us, whether through the Bible, prayer, teaching or prophecy, is glorifying the name of Christ and drawing us closer to our Father. It's clear that God is madly in love with us and will stop at nothing to reveal His heart for His Church and our lives.

THE GIFT OF TONGUES

You don't have to travel very far from your home to find people who speak differently from the way you do. Different families, different jobs, different cultures and different languages all have their own unique words and phrases. If you're an outsider, you may find the differences amusing—at least until you can't order a meal or find a place to stay for the night (see 1 Corinthians 14:10-11).

The words you speak connect you with others. Think about you and your friends. There's a good chance you have some words or phrases that only you and your friends know the meaning of. In a way, it's your own special language. Police officers, doctors, lawyers and football players have their own ways of speaking that

bring them together with others like them (see 1 Corinthians 14:2-4,14-15,18).

In the same way, the gift of tongues is a special language that some refer to as a prayer language. If anyone were to listen and try to make sense of what the words mean, he or she would be left scratching his or her head. That's because this gift is meant to be a private language between the speaker of tongues and God.

Most of the time, even the person speaking in tongues can't understand what he or she is saying. It is a language used when words just aren't enough. Maybe you're so moved or weighed down by a situation that you don't even know what to pray for or what words to use. Maybe you're so moved by God's love and holiness in a time of worship that no words can express the way you feel (see Romans 8:26). It's not the only sign that a person being filled with the Holy Spirit, nor is it a badge of holiness. It's another very intimate way of communicating with the Father.

Unlike prophecy, this gift is for use between one person and God. However, there are times in prayer ministry during which you may be led to pray in tongues.

If the person with whom you're praying doesn't understand the gift of tongues, explain a little about the gift so that he or she understands what is happening. As you pray, know that God is hearing and understanding your requests. Be sure that as you pray in tongues, you are open to what the Lord is saying as well and that you are ready to say anything He might ask you to say in your primary language.

Some may be confused about the gift of tongues: how do they receive it, what is its purpose and how do they know it's from God? Some might think of it as a gift only for the most spiritual of Christians. However, it's just one of many spiritual gifts God offers us. We only need to ask with the belief that we will receive. In other words, we need to ask with faith. To many, tongues may look like nonsense. The first time the Holy Spirit moved men and women to use this gift, many who heard them speaking thought they were drunk (see Acts 2:1-13).

Regardless of what people may think, the Bible makes it clear that the gift of tongues is meant as a powerful way for our hearts to pray to God. We shouldn't be hard on ourselves if it does not come right away, because not everybody will receive the gift of tongues. As we continue to ask for this gift, we can be sure God hears us and appreciates our desire to know Him better.

CHAPTER SIX

GOING DEEPER

We hope you have found this book helpful. Our prayer is that we will all be better equipped to serve God in the area of prayer ministry, both in the church and in our everyday lives.

For further reading about prayer or prayer ministry, we suggest the following books:

- Ahn, Ché. *How to Pray for Healing*. Ventura, CA: Regal Books, 2003.

- Campbell, Wesley. *Praying the Bible*. Ventura, CA: Regal Books, 2003.

- Collins, Bruce. *Prophesy!* Eastbourne, England: Kingsway, 2000.

- Pytches, David. *Come Holy Spirit*. London: Hodder and Stoughton, 1994.

- Sheets, Dutch. *Intercessory Prayer*. Ventura, CA: Regal Books, 1997.

If Soul Survivor can be of further help in equipping you or your church, please do not hesitate to contact us at info@soulsurvivor.com. Other Soul Survivor publications you may find helpful are now available from your local Christian bookstore, from Gospel Light at 1-800-4-GOSPEL, or online at www.soulsurvivor.com and www.gospellight.com.

A RADICALLY NEW WAY TO REACH YOUNG PEOPLE

soulsurvivor
encounter

If you want to inspire and equip young people, **Soul Survivor Encounter** is the key. Originating in England, Soul Survivor has released young leaders for Christ by teaching them about worship, action evangelism and social justice.

With **Soul Survivor Encounter**, you can use the successful elements of the Soul Survivor ministry to create in your young people a passionate commitment to worshiping God and putting their faith into action.

This biblical and relevant program is sure to ignite a revolution in youth ministry that will impact generations to come. Be a part of it!

Soul Survivor Kit
5 *Real Life & Undignified Worship Student Magazines*, 1 *Real Life & Undignified Worship Leader's Guide*, 1 *Real Life & Undignified Worship DVD*, *Soul Survivor Guide to Youth Ministry*, *Soul Survivor Prayer Ministry* and *Soul Survivor Guide to Service Projects*.
ISBN 08307.35267

Real Life & Undignified Worship Student Magazine
ISBN 08307.35364

Real Life & Undignified Worship Leader's Guide
ISBN 08307.35313

Real Life & Undignified Worship DVD
UPC 607135.008927

Soul Survivor Guide to Youth Ministry
ISBN 08307.35305

Soul Survivor Prayer Ministry
ISBN 08307.35275

Soul Survivor Guide to Service Projects
ISBN 08307.35291

Soul Survivor Encounter is available at your local Christian bookstore.

Gospel Light

More Breakthrough Books from Soul Survivor

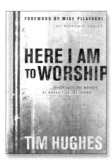

Here I Am to Worship
Never Lose the Wonder of
Worshiping the Savior
Tim Hughes
ISBN 08307.33221

Soul Sister
The Truth About
Being God's Girl
Beth Redman
ISBN 08307.32128

Soul Survivor
Finding Passion and Purpose
in the Dry Places
Mike Pilavachi
ISBN 08307.33248

**Pick up a copy at your
favorite Christian bookstore!
www.regalbooks.com**

Visit www.regalbooks.com to
join Regal's FREE e-newsletter.
You'll get useful excerpts from
our newest releases and special
access to online chats with your
favorite authors. Sign up today!

Regal
God's Word for Your World™

Take Worship to the Next Level!

The Unquenchable Worshipper
Coming Back to the Heart of Worship
Matt Redman
ISBN 08307.29135

The Heart of Worship Files
Featuring Contributions by Some of Today's Most Experienced Lead Worshippers
Matt Redman, General Editor
ISBN 08307.32616

Facedown
When you face up to God's glory, you find yourself facedown in worship.
Matt Redman
ISBN 08307.32462

Pick up a copy at your favorite Christian bookstore!
www.regalbooks.com

Visit www.regalbooks.com to join Regal's FREE e-newsletter. You'll get useful excerpts from our newest releases and special access to online chats with your favorite authors. Sign up today!

Regal
God's Word for Your World™